The Rhubarb King

Also by the same author

Different Arrangements

But I Won't Go Out in a Boat

A Stranger in Her House

The Other Mozart

The Rhubarb King

poems by

Sharon Chmielarz

Loonfeather Press
Bemidji, Minnesota

Copyright © 2006 by Sharon Chmielarz
All rights reserved

Cover Art: "Rain in May" by Andrei Andreevich Tutunov, oil on canvas, 1956. Provided by The Museum of Russian Art, 5500 Stevens Avenue South, Minneapolis, MN 55419.

First printing 2006
Printed in Canada by Hignell Book Printing
ISBN 0-926147-22-6

The author wants to thank Betty Rossi, Gail Rixen and Mary Lou Marchand for their invaluable help.

Thanks, too, to the Jerome Foundation for a travel grant which enabled several of these poems to be written and to editors along these poems' way and the editorial advice freely given by my writing group and friends.

This project is made possible, in part, by a grant from the Region 2 Arts Council through funding by the Minnesota State Legislature.

Loonfeather Press is a not-for-profit small press organized under section 501 (c) (3) of the United States Internal Revenue Code.

The Rhubarb King is printed on 100 percent recycled material including 20 percent post-consumer waste. This acid-free paper is oxygen-bleached, an environmentally friendly process.

Loonfeather Press
P.O. Box 1212
Bemidji, MN 56619

To Theodore

"Nobody remembers their names today,
And yet their hands were real once..."
Czeslaw Milosz

Acknowledgments

The following poems have been previously published:

The Rhubarb King in *Salmagundi*
The Steppe/Prairie in *Borealis*
In a Russian Garden in *Lake Street Review*
Getting Through Siberia; So-So Garden in *The Wolf Head Quarterly*
Long Distance Skating; German Russians from the Photo Album; Bessarabia in North Dakota; Rosina in *North Dakota Quarterly*
TEA in *The Artful Dodge*
Where the Radish Blooms in *Rhino*
Cold Lightning in North Dakota in *Louisiana Literature*
Letter from God to Eve in *Slant*
Last Look at the Deck in *Nimrod*
What He Handled or The Feel of Things in *Ascent*
Duet in the Little Blue Church in *Barrow Street*
Weispfennig House; Head on Heels; North Dakota Estate Sale; Vinegar; Reading the General's Envelope in *Poetry Northwest*
Remembering the Acts Done to the Dead; Washing My Face in *Poet Lore*
Garden; Gardener (Zinnia; Shade) in *Spoon River Review*
Windows; Floors in *Great River Review*
Meadowlarks in *ArtWord Quarterly*
Shed (Dream Room # 19) in *100 Words*
In His Car in *Abraxis*
The Clock in *Northeast*
So Far and No Farther in *Hurricane Alice*
A World of Its Own in *Minnesota Poetry Calendar*
Watching Two Crows Circle in *Minnesota Monthly*
Concert at the Countess's House (At a Concert Outside St. Petersburg) in *Exquisite Corpse*
Her Trunk in *Loonfeather*

Contents

The King

The Rhubarb King ~ 3

Duet in the Little Blue Church ~ 5

What He Handled or The Feel of Things ~ 6

Washing My Face ~ 7

Vinegar ~ 8

Long Distance Skating, North Dakota, 1910 ~ 9

In His Car ~ 10

In a Russian Garden

From the Photo Album: The German Russians, Their Houses ~ 13

Meadowlarks ~ 16

Rosina, 1890 ~ 17

In a Russian Garden ~ 19

TEA ~ 20

The Steppe/Prairie ~ 21

Getting Through Siberia ~ 22

To Lenin: On the Occasion of the November 7, 1916 Anniversary ~ 23

The Sacrifice ~ 24

Where the Radish Blooms ~ 25

Concert at the Countess's House ~ 26

Bessarabia in North Dakota ~ 27

So Far and No Farther ~ 28

Rooms

Rooms ~ 33
Garden ~ 35
Reading the General's Envelope ~ 37
Letter from God to Eve About the Annual Yield ~ 39
Hands ~ 40
So-So Garden ~ 41
Head on Heels ~ 42
Remembering the Acts Done to the Dead ~ 43
Cold Lightning in North Dakota ~ 44
A World of Its Own: Cabbage ~ 45
Watching Two Crows Circle ~ 46
Final Statements ~ 47
Things ~ 48
Thinking of the Past's Usefulness ~ 49
Weispfennig House, Fredonia, North Dakota ~ 50
North Dakota Estate Sale, 1965 ~ 51
Bread, 1908 ~ 53
Her Trunk ~ 54
Last Look at the Porch ~ 55
Clock ~ 57
The Old Man Makes It ~ 58
Morning Glories ~ 59
Sky and Moon ~ 60

The King

The Rhubarb King

The rhubarb king sits in the garden,
resting under the arms of a hackthorn,

that ancient tree, while the court photographer—
my sister, his daughter—snaps him there.

His curved-handled cane leans
like a good dog against his leg.

His cap is slanted, his cheeks shaved,
his moustache—once fine and black, sleek

and mean has turned into an old king's
cowcatcher. His eyes, guarded, defying,

run to blue, as if his kingdom was not
always as bountiful or beautiful as wanted,

not as smashing as the rhubarb stalks
he grips, like nightsticks, giant, leaf-topped

scepters on his left and right, clubs that
furl into heart-shapes; toxic, oil-tough

with ruffled edges. Like the kingdom
I ran from.

In the window behind this instant,
among suncatchers and a row of snakeplants

withering in crockery, I see the ethereal
form in the palace, the rhubarb queen.

I can make out a wing, her chest,
her garlanded head. She's

peering past the king as if calling,
calling for her hands. His are there, brown,

strong. How is she to make something
sweet of his kingdom, without hands?

And hers were dear, very dear and deft.
—My sister, long after the king's death,

sends me this photo. I take it upon myself
to write the caption: *All history is myth.*

Duet in the Little Blue Church

Listening to him,
you'd think we two sang
the way the saved sing,
making the connection
between loss and love,
holding its music,
cracking stars,
my dad's bass to my alto.

Listening to him,
you'd think sorrow
our beacon,
joy the rose
light on snow.

You'd even think
disappointment,
sitting in the back pew,
unfrozen from frowning,
had opened a mouth, as echo.

What He Handled or The Feel of Things

He liked clout, weight, silver—coins
kept in the black steel box under the kitchen
floorboards. His ring, size 14, sported
a dance-red stone on the club of his hand.
I never asked the undertaker how he got the thing off,
I just stashed it away in a drawer.

He used to change after work in the powerplant,
from sweaty twills to smooth pleasure,
a cotton cowboy shirt, fake pearl snaps.
He liked fleshy, Mae West women, the hard curve
of a steering wheel, a hymnal's spine,
a magazine whose cover oozed fear and blood.

He picked his teeth with a toothpick—Yup—
called any machine "she," pared his nails
with a knife, smoked Camels, drank, played
whist in the back of the Arcade, used his mean
tone when slapping down the ace. *Let's see that
sonafabitch trump me now.*

Dad even liked handling Mom's Kirby,
pushing her over the carpet, roaring over
any violence left in the house. The dustrag
crumpled in his ample palm as he wiped off
the coffeetable, around and over the Bible,
lying there like a big, fat knick-knack to look at.

He never got over the feel of things.
When he was old, he took up a pen, that
awkward, little tool. On family-tree pages
he printed in names and dates, strikemarks
on a thin, papery wall, showing he'd been here,
made some elbow room on his way passing through.

Washing My Face

This morning when I cupped my hands to rinse my face,
when I lifted them, eyes closed,
the image they carried
up out of nowhere, out of the water, after all these years,
that same old thing,
my father, bent over,
beating my mother; her twisted face. Bent over
the sink, hands dripping, I waited
for the scene to pass, all the while shaking.
That this can keep coming up.
That this can keep coming up.
That my own hands keep bringing it up
out of the well.

Vinegar

My mother's kind. For recipes known by hand.
I see her at the counter, stirring,
a presence in the corner of an eye and
not quite there either, rather somewhere, near.

*The house, warm from the oven, the back door
open, something made with soured milk baking.
(Curds you'd never drink, kept in a coffee cup.)
In the alchemy of vinegar, it will taste sweeter.*

She didn't let things spoil on purpose.
She used, makeshift, what had happened.
Measured it out from a blue drinking cup,
asked the bitter to rise and taste better.

Long Distance Skating, North Dakota, 1910

He skated at recess, downhill from the schoolhouse.
He hunched down at ice edge, strapped blades to his boots,
took a shaky glide onto the lake (a marshy pond in a lee)
and sailed on coat corners in a northwest wind,
the whole, great idea of speed and flight enchanting to a boy
bound by gravity. Soon classmates joined him,
and then there were nine dark-clothed skaters
in winter black on white, scoring a continent and a day
otherwise hemmed in by land and its chores of husbandry.

Helpless, the old man recalling the scene can only watch
the kids pull the boy from a hole of floating ice-cakes and
wobble like crows on blades from lake to schoolhouse.
Wind almost rips the school door out of their hands, my
dad tastes again the sweaty haste in closing it, he must
smell again the school room's odor, extinct now, a barn-like
soiled-bedclothes collection of heat, soot, sweat, and woolen
underwear stained by urine. He must hear again the teacher,
the older girl, scold in English his dripping arrival into her room.
Ice flaked off the pants she peeled down his shaking legs.

"Such a thing!" My dad shames himself for skating, for falling
through thin ice—how did he never get whipped for that!
"I don't know how it was I never got sick from that," he says.
"I could'uf drowned. Died." My dad shakes his head
over the unknown words in the boy's vocabulary,
and the present clears, forgiving in its forgetfulness
the closet of a room, the pile of blades at its door. Today
he'll warm himself by eating what he's fixed for Sunday dinner.
That means noon. A meal for one. Frozen Banquet chicken.
What do you call 'em?—French fries. Ja. They hit the spot.
Easy to warm up in the oven. Easy to clean up on his own.

In His Car

My father's driving down 83, from North
to South Dakota. "Full moon out,"
he tells me later on the phone.
"Big as he can be. No wind.
No cars on the road. Just go, go."

On the road under the moon
my father has not yet met his conqueror,
some superior death machine,
motionless and moonless. He goes
undefeated in his kingdom, which I can find

listed only in my records.

In a Russian Garden

From the Photo Album: The German Russians, Their Houses

Strongholds. Germans in Bessarabia, a region in eastern Moldavia, west of Odessa. Poor, ravished by Napoleon's swipes across their fields, they'd left Swabia to take up the old Tsarina's promise of free land, no taxes (for ten years), no military service.

Enclaves. They kept their language and customs and religion. When the Tsarina's grandson declared German colonies must learn Russian, must report for military service, they faked concessions; when he froze further accumulation of land, they emigrated to America.

Rolling house. Under the wagon bed the young woman (my grandmother) spent the winter. Cowchip and sod walls and the backs of her family in unison kept out the full blast of north wind.

Sod houses. Since there was no river through the land the immigrants took in the Dakota Territory, there were no trees. Since there was no wood to build with, the only thing left was a willingness to live on dirt, in dirt and from dirt.

Canvas. A boy might get 15¢ to take to the circus if it was a good year. He'd come back with 30¢. Born to work on the 4th of July. Save and work. Feed the elephant. Haul buckets of water. Shovel shit for the ringmaster. A ten-year-old German Russian was used to it.

Dark houses. Except on winter nights darkness was a hands-on experience. A moonless night penetrated silence, the fields, the rise where the farm sat. Essence of darkness curtained the dirt hut's kerosene lamp on the shadowed crate.

Rich houses. When they were all not poor anymore—when people are poor then all should share—all did not help a neighbor put up a barn or clap sideboards on the sod house. Or hang a door, a strip of boards good as paper against winter wind. When they were no longer poor, all did not thresh or help with the header at harvest. All began to pay a hired man. It was the end of calling, the beginning of whispered muttering.

The English houses. A German Russian, pronounced *German Roosian*, goes to the back door to knock on a house which is not of his class.

God's house. The tremendous effort of being a Baptist in a dry land! How much easier the Catholics and Lutherans had it—even a child could find a teaspoon of water to sprinkle over a forehead. No running water in the church (to this day), but once a year the Baptists filled the whole baptistery.

Swedes' houses. German Russians lived south of town. Swedes, north. "We thought they was dirty guys. Filthy guys," Uncle Karl recalls. "I can't remember what they thought of us. I got to know some Swedish people and they was nice people. But they lived different."

Shaded houses. Aunt Edda threatened to cut down the tree outside her kitchen window in town. "It makes the kitchen too dark. Oh, when I think of the time that tree was no bigger than my finger!" She looked at the circumference of her bony index finger with regret and longing. "Then I could have gone out there and cut it down myself." She's lived under hot, steppe-like sun over eighty years, no trees close to her farmhouse, no trees in the fields. You'd think she'd be hungry for shade, for the comfort of shadow. But no. She wants no part of ease. She wants to go out of her house into a blast of light, everything too hot, too flaming to look directly into its face; no shadows to hide among or protect the mushroom whiteness of the skin she has always kept covered from direct heat and light.

House as clock. Grandfather Gottlieb never wore a watch. A fob never dangled from his vest. Not on work clothes. Six days a week when he was at work in his fields, if he wanted to know the time he straightened up and looked toward his house, measuring the depth of shade falling from the eaves. It didn't matter which season, which shadows were longer or shorter; he knew what time it was. Even on cloudy days, Grandfather was never wrong.

House as shaft. I drive up a slope; before me, across the entire valley's fields and accompanying set of hills, arches a rainbow. The largest rainbow I've ever seen, that I can remember, spans the prairie's infinite curve. One pillar's footing is lost in gray cloud, but the other towers free. Everything in the shadow of the bow's colored scrim turns pink and gold—alchemy through crowns of trees; grains and grasses filtered into radiance. Look what God has made. Look what man has made, from fields begotten on filched deeds. What a shaft.

Paternal house. Although my dad did the best he could—his apologia after my mother's death—he dies a failure. Not a classic failure, for print ignored reporting any phase of his life; and not in the eyes of the town's high muckymucks, for they lent him on the subject of success not a glance of consideration—but in his own mind he'd failed. Far more devastating. Note the drama roiling in the spectacular cloud over his shack's roof.

Meadowlarks

A long winter
alone in his house,
his four-room shack,
now it's March.

He leaves the kitchen
radio blaring and
walks outside
to listen

in his hutch of a body,
for the snowy
land to melt
under five-notes—

the first meadowlark,
returned to its post
on the plains, somewhere
along the railroad track.

On the phone, later,
he's yellow-throated,
making territorial calls.
"We're all waiting

for spring,"
he cheers, as if I am
as sure in spring
as the lark to return.

Rosina, 1890

She'll take a chance on the Czar,
who's losing patience with the German colonists,
their unwillingness to serve
in his army, their protestations over land taxes,
their open-mouthed disbelief
at being told to learn Russian. Speak Russian?
She'll stay behind, unable to conceive
the history on its way: the Revolution, Lenin, WW II.
In her blue-washed rooms,
she'll keep the thirteen days in the year
her brothers lose by traveling to America.
She'll sleep in a clean bed and close the evening
window on the *Dreshplatz*/threshing floor,
and the dog barking in her valley in Bessarabia.
She'll never expect a letter; letters were most rare.
But she'll hear, over the years, from the pastor,
who could read a bit, tales of ox-cart trips,
through grass taller than a horse, over
ruts in trails that led to the eventual
banker dickering over 36% interest on a loan.
Rosina at her little, clothed table will have pleasure
knowing she has saved the entrance fee,
ten American dollars, and the land officer's
four dollars by staying in the U.S.S.R. After the war,
she'll die for free, among the first, the old, the Germans
taken from their communes and starved under Stalin.
Which is why Rosina isn't among the 19th Century
immigrants crowding the train's exits after a two weeks' trip
from Castle Garden to Dakota Territory, getting their legs
back on Menno's Main Street, stopping at the saloon

for a bucket of beer. Her brothers peer into a livery's
open door, as I do, decades later, in the footsteps
of my father's family. On this late October day,
grease monkeys sprawl over fenders with the idle
ease of stable boys on Friday. I walk on to Town Hall,
entrance off Main, up one flight of stairs.
Closed. Like the museum.
So I browse the town library for more history.
The library is the high school's study hall.
A few shelves on the wall. Well, what did I expect?
Germans from Russia wanted land, not books.
They were swayed by a field or a charlatan, never
by an intellectual. That they had in common with the Czar,
whose macrocosm is this library's microcosm: I watch
a student break a petty, thoughtless rule.
The teacher overreacts; as sudden as gunshot,
the student's a troublemaker and a victim. His peers
line up behind him, a mass of jeering faces, acting out
the history of tyrants. Like Rosina in old age, I haven't
a stomach for it anymore. I close the jubilee book,
slip out of the room, her voice in my ears, glad
to leave, God, yes, whatever the cost, let's move on.

In a Russian Garden

This evening I saw my father
on a bench in the garden's shade.
I saw him easily from the gate.
I said to myself, I'll draw him out.
Father, I called from the gate,
give me a fish, I am hungry.
And I held out my bag for a scorpion.
Father, I called again from the gate,
give me bread for my journey.
And I held out my bag for a stone.
I called, Father, kiss me
and held my hanky ready
to wipe the spittle off my cheek.
Slowly he rose from the bench.
He took my bag and filled it
from the evening's dark rows.
He hugged me once,
over the gate between us,
and gave back the sack.
It bulged with proof.
I hurried to my friend's house,
dumped the bag on her table—
out rolled cabbages, cucumbers, tomatoes.
My friend's eyes rolled up to heaven.
She didn't believe.
Lies! Lies! I cried. Again
he hasn't given me what I need!
No stones! No scorpions.

TEA

Samovar and parquet floor,
pasque flower in a jar,
the maid's spotless headband,
embroidered rim of her white apron,
chapped elbows, cracked gray clay . . .

in the fields of Moldavia,
in Pushkin's house, at his table,
we drank tea this afternoon—
ancient sentence, "We drank tea."
And how we lived to tell it.

The Steppe/Prairie

Not the garden of your dreams!
Like a train, the steppe heads east.
The steppe heads west.
Its silence shakes
your bedroom window
late at night. And just
as you lie breathless
in its roar, when any
second could be
snapped in two, the
steppe dies down.
You're the one,
breathing hard,
calling it kind
for not crushing you.

Getting Through Siberia

Beside the tracks, a gypsy wagon.
I push aside the maroon door drape—
souvenir dolls dangle from the ceiling
by strings around their necks. I

leave quickly, board the train,
dream the steppe rolling past
Line 1 to the end, the last stop,
a lightplant, a fortress

in a forest of watts.
I press the door buzzer.
It sets the night shrilling.
A tower answers, flashing

light in sections,
showering me
in the language of gulags
and baseball diamonds.

To Lenin: On the Occasion of the November 7, 1916 Anniversary

After you're dead things happen
the way they do in dreams.
Without legs you parade
through every factory
you never stepped into in real life.
Somebody buttonholes you hero,
hangs your photo over a turbine,
makes you into god.

Not every worker's converted.
In the night more than one
Tsarist babushka weeps
in her feathertick for the good
old days when Red picture-paste-ups
didn't moon the streets,
when stars didn't ooze
a stream of blood.

The Sacrifice
(based on "The Coming Storm" by Martin Johnson Heade, 1859)

Not much time left and not much light.
When the clouds crush that last
coppery pendant, sky and lake
will be one explosion—doom—end
of the man's picnic, his flasks
awash on the altar of a rock.

Like grace before a meal,
the sailboat's "L" swings unworried,
though the rower, nearer shore,
is the sort who has nothing
to give but himself, and thus more
expendable in a priestly act.

How awful if we had to watch,
the head held down like a dog's
underwater, and listen
to a fatherly voice, shredded
by anger and fear, praying
he never has to save us again.

Where the Radish Blooms

Where the radish blooms
(gone to seed in a garden beside the Neva),
a toddler, munching bread
on the pebbled path, follows the babushka's
black club heels.

Heels that believe
in pounding, in chores that must be
done because Work is
sweet as salted radish on bread, radish sliced
round as kopeks.

The black heels stop
at the Neva's crumbling bank: time for a picnic.
"Eat, dear child.
Eat it all up and watch your motherland
swell with blossom."

Concert at the Countess's House

Except for one oddity—the lone
lean descendant from nobility—

the musicians are granddaughters
of serfs, and a godmother

has turned a pumpkin into the State's
conductor, who, in turn, waves

her baton—one, and—music fills the ballroom
in the manor: Songs by Borodin,

Rimsky-Korsakov, Tschaikovsky,
composers the Countess heartily

disdained long before the night she pitched
the manor's keys into the pack

of rabble stinking up her boudoir.
(The ring only grazed a proletarian ear.)

Last seen in the bead of a gun, the Countess
was fleeing through her French doors,

now ours, running over the parterre
into the garden's rows of sculpted cedar.

Tonight the inheritors squat on the ribs
of her gilded, nineteenth-century chairs.

The music builds under her roof a little house,
a fiction we're as good as the old guard was.

Of course, they weren't.
Of course, we are.

Bessarabia in North Dakota

Each tree trunk in the lane lined with acacias
is painted white, pretty as horse legs,
lusty but domestic, sprung from seeds,
a gift from Count Richelieu.

Sometimes a villager appears on the lane,
from the houses that squat like men's hats.
Sometimes tame geese stroll at her feet.
They are past the last peeling slat

in the picket fence, on the worn path
to the well. An old man is the early bird,
in billy cap, already filling his plastic bucket.
Crows sit on a high wire, cawing and flying up

when the white horse pulls a wagon by
on tires. Two black calves raise their voices.
One scarlet-combed rooster and two fat hens
squawk *orange! orange!* under pink acacias.

And what are the other colors of the lost?
Half moons and grape vines and morning glory clusters,
bachelor buttons escaped from gardens, diamonds
on housetiles in old woman yellows, lavender and blues.

So Far and No Farther

But I go farther than the visa permits.
Past towns with names I can't pronounce,
past billy clubs and bureaucratic warnings,
I drive so far out no hotel will take me in:
Strangers out here aren't welcome
for the trouble they bring.

What do I care?
I'm a muzhik,
dizzy in the head
after two glasses of *kvas*.
I coast downhill, ignition
turned off, saving petrol.

The car slows. The road
becomes a slough. A tractor
couldn't make it through this
muck. Where's the KGB
when you need them? I'm
stuck. Shit. I get out and walk,

lose a shoe.
Just like a kid;
the very pair
Father
worked so hard for.
You drove into this mud, now *you* . . .

Down the road a piece
I see a hut. I knock.
Birds pip warnings. One
beady eye peeks out a slit.
"Who are you?" A croak, behind
the door. "What do you want?"

It's so easy in Russia to know who I am.
I'm an American. I want a room.
I'm cold and hungry, frustrated.
My car's stuck in a nightmare.
—Babushka! Mama! Jesus
has commanded you to take me in.

Rooms

Rooms

Moon

Moon comes early to the bedroom, to the mirror
of the man with the heavy-lidded eye. His bed doubles
in the reflection, glass filming, milking what will happen:
Moon crawling on her belly, all the way across the earth,
to offer him her robe and bathe his feet in light.

Key

Maybe this isn't his house—the key doesn't fit.
Is it a place in the country? Are we under earth,
in a cellar? At the foot of the stairs someone has
planted a tree, such long strands of leaves.
Like the girl ". . . who's thrown her hair before her,
over her head to dry in the sun." Translucent,
shining in the dark down here.

Windows

His are old, puffy as eyelids, the paint peels
like dried sleep, windows in need of washing.
They're fine if you don't touch them. But tap
with a hammer—top left, bottom right—to straighten
the warp, and you'd make it worse. You might even
smash the glass. Then what would you do, your dad
and you, with so much light inside the house?

Closet

The music composed for this room mourns the gray
skeleton inside, weathered as a stripped tree, torn
from its bed underground. The whole closet goes gray
with separation. A gray wail. Now his house isn't empty.

Bedroom

The house is arty, the lawn's a picnic, little round tables
and strolling guests. If my dad's out driving his 88 Olds,
he'll run right into this, smudged glasses and all. Where is he,
anyway? I peek upstairs in the bedroom—find him asleep
among the coats, his body a spoon to loneliness. Armless
pillow for her dead body. My mother's wig, for her head.

Floors

Mine are glass. If you lift the rug's edge, you can see
down through all the stories. How can glass floors be safe?
These barely, barely hold me. Other renters skim over
their glass floors. They're rich, slim, young as Dad's undertaker,
everything pinned and buttoned down. They party. They sing,
"No problem!" Didn't they see my dad fall? Didn't they see
how his arms flew up—toward me—in surrender?

Attic

And this is the attic, this long room. Its five windows,
wide open. A table with vase in the middle.
How has the bouquet survived all winter? In the draft,
these peonies sprawl like an elm. Pale, ready to fly
Chagall-like out the windows, out of town, over hills
of terracotta roofs, a flock of blue petals imitating
clouds, leaving the Box Mountains behind.

Hold

Someone's filling his house with water—turning the rooms
into dead pools. I'm sitting to the side, on a slope in the yard,
trying to decide how this can be when the house begins to sink.
Maybe this is how the ocean rises. Maybe, how it weeps.

Garden

Bramble

Look what blooms under this bramble cleared of weeds—
a tumble of blue falling down on weepy stems. Overgrown
Someday flattened under rain. And more on the way.
The petals tremble, rain-pocked. The blue glistens.

Zinnia

So much room here on the north side, but shade makes
such a miserable garden, so skimpy, a zinnia just ups and
walks away. Where is the one who can help, who listens
to a garden, as you might listen to a heartbeat?
Parched gumbo skin; the face, a house of north and south
passages; ears, like yours and mine, caves; eyes, grottos.
In the recesses, a blue mirage of light.

Shed

We have a wonderful house in the city, but I discover
in a garden another smaller, more wonderful house.
A potting shed. Or summerhouse. The door's ajar.
Vines trellis the lintel. But, oh! The flower pots!
The dirt is dead dry. What a wonder the flowers
bloom at all, these faded japonica.

Shade

Of course we feared someone trashing the house
after he died. And before he died we feared he'd be
mugged in his own living room, an easy armchair target:
a widower hustling Seagrams by night; by day, an old man
pruning the hedge, alone in his garden. —The trees!
What if the trees he planted are gone, too?
The shade they give the house!
I quick pull on my shoes and run out to see
all manner of creatures gathered under the ash.
A fawn in a lawn chair, and a woman growing
from the ground. She grows as tall as a child
before she leaves his shade to me.

Reading the General's Envelope

My dad carries his war lightly now,
stuffed in his shirt pocket,

and drives it to the post office,
an after-dinner habit, dropping

a little bomb of a letter off.
The name and address

on this one are mine.
Poked out on his Underwood.

Orders in upper and lower case,
sputtered periods and commas

scattered like buckshot
over the envelope's white field,

open grounds for more
pounding on—more wildlife

stamp displays. His genre
of belle lettres. *Lick & bam.*

On the back side,
under the sealed V

for victory, a postscript
parades his third grade

education and shaky
hand: MEDOWLARK SANG

ON RAILROAD TRACK THIS MORNING.
Sang between us, in code,

how much cannot be named,
how much I've missed.

Letter from God to Eve About the Annual Yield

Last year, He writes, His trees bore two apples.
This year, so many *they look like grape trees.*
(He's creating again, things that never were.)
He has, in His terrible spelling and archaic accent,
two *laidys* come and carry away the windfall. His own
garbage can is full and there's *enoughter* pailful
falling even now as He sits at the table, typing, cross-
breeding words of multiple syllables and meanings.

Last year, Eve read His letters with dry eyes.
This year, with tears. Why, why this sadness
over bounty? Why miss an apple man and wish
you were the lady helping Him with the windfall?
Why ache for pailfuls of sweet, rotten fruit?
Her tears dry. She likes the business-like way
He signs His name, first and last (He has no middle),
God the Father, and then adds the folksy title, "Dad."

Hands

We have identical hands, my father and I.
Extra large, hard to find gloves for.
My father folds his out of habit
when the Preacher prays.

A mass on his belly.
A belief in the Testaments' yoke,
a scripture of rest and work.
Unfolded they return to chores.

Incredible inventions they are.
Our constant song, that anyone
should have been so smart
to have thought of making hands!

Must have been a German.
Like peasants we tend ours, oiling
and binding the bruises with a barn-like
collection of funnels and rags.

We'll never throw our hands away.
When we visit, we keep them in boxes,
avoiding accidental touch, but look:
Yours. Mine. Worlds. Within reach.

So-So Garden

Their parsnips, long white rat tails.
The carrots, a row of mole's teeth.
The peppers, collapsed pouches.
Radishes, like the marriage, gone to seed.

Early on in the season they gave up
on the cucumber hills. And the beets
never grew past the size of cats' hearts.

Something got into the tomatoes
and turned the turnips to wood,
though the neighbor's squash did well.
They hated squash.

They made it through the winter
on Uncle Gus's red potatoes.
Theirs wasn't the only failure.

The same rain fell on everyone
in this valley and beyond.
The same, in the good gardens
beyond and beyond them.

Head on Heels

Fallen in love again—"head on heels"—
with the same woman, his life had turned
upside down. Could this house still be his,
this snowed-in winter shed, when the walls

ached to bloom? His door was still a door,
though knobs turned backwards. Windows
opened from the top. The roof pooled,
the postbox stuck its tongue out to get

a taste of snowflake. Even the grating
gate latch challenged the new order,
complaining all night to yellow stars
where his love, my mother, resides.

And he, poor man, slept on the ceiling;
all his floors had rolled into corners.
Everything cupboard-wise swam topsy-
swervy. Everything he fixed boiled under.

His chair was a cave he longed to visit but
he was waiting for a windgust from the south.
She would return on it, she must, and set
the house to rights again, heels on head.

Remembering the Acts Done to the Dead

Then my dad measured time
from the day of my mother's death.
To get out he attended funerals.

At the latest, he said, not one
big shot showed up. "And they're
supposed to be good people."

Good people remember the dead.
They follow the cop on the motorcycle,
little orange fender flags fluttering.

They lunch afterwards at the church,
at rows of paper-covered tables
that rasp with the weight of what is

coming. Only the Departed
can refuse the Ladies Aide Circle,
hushed offerings of sympathy

and judgment—green jello, white
bread. It lumps in the mouth.
Good people sit down and swallow.

Cold Lightning in North Dakota

Like the road, the music bridges miles
and fields, flooded in late spring, a long,
cold spring, but listening to Telemann while
driving away makes everything warm
as cold lightning—That bolt that struck
Fredonia's Martin Luther Church?
That was cold, that wasn't hot,
hot would have set it on fire. Cold
only thrilled the walls
and the timbre of Aunt Bertha's voice.
Cold made the church glad to be found
by God, that Poke and Rod, who wakes
stones up before letting them fall
back, sparked, sealed into place.

A World of Its Own: Cabbage

A cabbage, a perfect cabbage,
the most perfect cabbage they've ever seen,
absolutely perfect, people say

at the county fair. A cabbage
grown by the woman hunched
on the three-legged stool.

After the evening fireworks
men drink to her cabbage
before leaving the inn, before going

downhill home, smelling plowed
earth in fields and their own humble
cabbage soup kept warm on the stove.

Watching Two Crows Circle

Hunger is strong and curious. Defiant, won't move.
It is snow midway up the cornstalk.
It is morning. It is frost on a field of thistle.
Morning frost across a field of weeds.
It is a black peck in the snow with no kernel of corn
forthcoming.
It is the field oak's bare height.
It is a field the deer have gleaned.
A crazy shag of black wings through weeds,
a shunt through watery hoarfrost.
It is the screaming and warning "I!"
It is for corn, through corn, in corn.
It is stomach. It is one seeking trinity.

Final Statements

Leftovers from his desk,
a box of relics, final
statements. To be
taken care of, put away
like a naked photo.

A halting pair of hands,
mine, moves over this
last business, like eyes
being informed
of muscle and bone.

Only one box?
In life he preferred
the whole story.
Bared could be its title.
Basta could be its end.

Things

Two things the house wanted:
another floor, another story.

Things haven't changed either
in the grove of Russian olives.

The lilacs barely make a green
dent in the toasted grass.

Yellow-headed blackbirds,
a-swirl, make it easy

to believe things
could go on forever. That

observation slips
in the front door with the dust.

Things go a little faster at the end,
when rooms disappear between laths.

Thinking of the Past's Usefulness

. . . of the hollow in the palm
that measured the salt
for a batch of bread;

of an afternoon nap
snitched on the couch
while a blind's drawstring

nicked against the north
window in rhythm to the sheer
curtain's billows. No one

starved in this usefulness.
He brought vegetables in
from the garden. She

did them up, chopping
on a wooden board that was
useful as morning itself,

useful as the child
sent to fetch a jar
from the cellar's shelves.

—"Your legs are younger than mine."—
Of great use in the past, on a hot
afternoon, that cool, deep closet.

Weispfennig House, Fredonia, North Dakota

You see how important a door can be,
its position, letting the known in,
keeping the unwanted out.
This one is a real soldier, black trim,
vintage 40s, employed to maintain quiet,
to swing on common sense alone.
No one has kicked this door around.

And after sixty years the screen
shimmers under sunlight, still
begging light into its skin. Light
obliges, stroking doorsill,
wooden, clean and varnished floor,
blue foot rug, too. And extends
a gentle hand toward kitchen.

A stiff little breeze wants to
come in, too. So do swallows
diving from eaves. The door struts
its belt of balusters, a waltz
of wooden, miniature pillars.
By midmorning I can see light has fallen
for the door and made herself a home.

North Dakota Estate Sale, 1965

Pump organ went fast,
Uncle Henry's kingdom of keys
and stops, down in the cellar,
land of one song
tamped by the hardwood house floors.
Grandpa himself hummed.

Hummed when he walked and
hummed when he rocked
beside the Copperclad coal and wood stove,
like new, in easy reach
of the kitchen where Grandma
rolled out noodle dough.

Grandpa sat like a guard at the parlor
door; no one inside
but a skinny hat tree and a fat maroon
davenport and chair, two small tables,
antique china-closet-combination-writing-desk.
I never saw it used for writing,

it was the roosting place
for the ceramic chicken
my dad wanted,
but Aunt Pauline got to first.
They never spoke again
to each other.

This bill of auction pretty well lists
everything in the house I ever saw ...
what's this Homestead sewing machine,
was it kept in the bedroom?
And the Philco table model radio?
I never once saw or heard that.

Heard the clock
marching in place, training
twenty-four hours a day,
heard the cellar song tamped by floorboards,
heard the rolling pin
thump the table. And the humming.

Bread, 1908
for Theodore, b. 1905; d. 1993

The table rocks when he bumps it.
Mother doesn't like that. She's making flour
snow into the bowl. He wants to crank

the sifter, too, and fold in bread's secret,
gray and doubling in the saucer.

Outside the sodhouse, the meadowlawk's
dipthonged song: *This yellow sash,
it will be lost.* Now she's kneading,

shaping, rounding, lining up loaves
like the houses in town. *"Wiehst du?"*

He nods, it's why he's stood so long
beside her, mouth-hungry for the bite
she pinches off. How warm its walls.

How light, how brief this kingdom.
How large the hand that loved him.

Her Trunk

arched open
in the farmhouse bedroom

in the morning, fell to
in the evening, marked time

by silence as clocks do
by balance, in a room

with one window, the eastern
opening on the fields'

daily advancement,
the night's retreat.

The trunk served also as couch
to the farmer's children, a live-in,

secure in its relegation
to the extremities of a room;

an enigma in a time when furniture's
bought to stay put. And married,

in the end, to cast-offs that hulk
in shadows around the furnace.

Last Look at the Porch

What bristle the broom has
left, has been swept
into a permanent mare's tail.

The cat likes to brush against
it and sun on the chair,
its cat-hair-covered cushion.

Parked beside the door
are the garden shoes, laceless
and stiff from spending too much time

in last September's rain and frost.
Along the railing, three pots crow
mossroses, marigolds and blue stars.

Another human touch: on a hanger
a pair of shorts dries al fresco in a corner.
Under an eave, the rainwater pot's

one-half inch full, as is the cat's
water dish (a tuna can).
Around it the porch floor's wet.

Should he come this afternoon,
when the backyard's summer-still
as if everything is napping,
should that grim thief come
for me, stepping purposefully up
each wooden step, his long, dark

sleeves belling and filling,
you'll know the things, the beloved
things he stole from my eyes.

Clock

Did he know
when he made it
how it would keep
time in my room?

No slowing, no
uneven breathing
like his, no
gaping silences—

as if I didn't
know how impossible
in a hospital
it is to hear actually

a man fall
to his death—
then his last breath.
But his clock,

with its good
battery, goes
on beating,
beating,

with a pulse
the same as mine,
regular,
wooden.

The Old Man Makes It

From his doorstep he can see a path
where snowdrifts are less deep, like
a trail along the slope of a mountain,
where, if you rely on poles and go slow,
you could climb it.
The old man vows he'll do it.
The old man with gray stubble on his chin.

Once he skirts the whale of a ridge,
the body that tails right up
to his house, then curls like a wave
or snarled lip, the rest will be easy.
With broomsticks, held broomhead up,
he'll scale it, with two old brooms,
planted like poles in the snow.

He can feel the wind raw
on the back of his legs,
as if he wore gauze.
Up slope, down slope, without
friendly back-up, across a world's
glacier to the garden shed, his base camp.
His breath huffs. His thumping heart cheers.

Morning Glories

This morning, three blue morning glories and the spirit
of my dead father urge me to drive west,
out to the marshland, wheatfields, drift prairie,
morning wind in the Moreau's cottonwoods.
I move slowly. Too slowly! He is ready,
already sitting, impatient! in the front seat.
His hands in mine, controlling the wheel;
his feet, in mine on the pedal.
He insists my eyes see.
"Look! Look! Ain't it beautiful!"

Sky and Moon

Go see what's doing in the apple cellar.
See what's making that rumbling.
See if someone's in the barrels
like a bear, gobbling down our work.
If it's a young man and you can love him,
fill him up on flesh and seed.
If he's down-and-out, tell him come-on-up;
in this house we eat in the kitchen.
If it's lazy Cousin Elsie, turn her away;
she can make do in her own apple cellar.
Then come tell me what you discover.
Tell me how much is gone, we'll count
what's left together, how much
we have to last the winter.

Photograph by Norbert Marklin

Sharon Chmielarz was born in Mobridge, South Dakota. She received a BS and an MA from the University of Minnesota and taught in the public schools for thirty years. She began writing after taking a course on the poetry of Auden and has since been published in many literary magazines in the United States, England and Canada

In 1981 and 1989 she won the Minnesota Voices Contest. Her first two books of Poetry were *Different Arrangements* and *But I Won't Go Out in a Boat* (New Rivers Press, 1982 and 1990). *The Other Mozart* was published by Ontario Review Press in 2001.

She lives in Minneapolis, Minnesota.